2005
DE
1

Kool Logic
La Lógica kool

Bilingual Press/Editorial Bilingüe

Publisher
  Gary D. Keller

Executive Editor
  Karen S. Van Hooft

Associate Editors
  Adriana Brady
  Brian Ellis Cassity
  Cristina de Isasi
  Linda St. George Thurston

Editorial Board
  Juan Goytisolo
  Francisco Jiménez
  Mario Vargas Llosa

Address:
Bilingual Press
Hispanic Research Center
Arizona State University
PO Box 875303
Tempe, Arizona 85287-5303
(480) 965-3867

Kool Logic
La lógica kool

poems by

Urayoán Noel

Bilingual Press/Editorial Bilingüe
Tempe, Arizona

ISBN 1-931010-29-3

Library of Congress Cataloging-in-Publication Data

Noel, Urayoán.
    Kool logic = La lógica kool / Urayoán Noel.
        p. cm.
    ISBN 1-931010-29-3
    1. Hispanic Americans—Poetry. I. Title: Lógica kool. II. Title.

    PS3614.O39K64 2004
    811'.6—dc22   2004054544

PRINTED IN THE UNITED STATES OF AMERICA

Front cover art: Little Gold Man *(1990) by Diane Gamboa*

Cover and interior design by Bill Greaves

Acknowledgments
This publication is supported by the Arizona Commission on the Arts with funding from the State of Arizona and the National Endowment for the Arts.

Arizona
Commission
on the Arts

NATIONAL
ENDOWMENT
FOR THE ARTS

Acknowledgments

Gracias to the following publications where a number of these poems first appeared: *Autana, Avenue Be, En la orilla, Long Shot, New York Quarterly, Poetry Motel, Roar Shock, Wavelength, Hostos Review, Mudfish, Los nuevos caníbales v. 2: antología de la más reciente poesía del Caribe hispano* (Isla Negra, 2003), and *eXpresiones: muestra de ensayo, teatro, narrativa, arte y poesía de la generación X* (Instituto de Cultura Puertorriqueña, 2003).

Thanks also to Virgil Suárez, Bob Holman, and everyone at Bilingual Press and at NYU. Por último, my love and gratitude go out to friends and family, to objet petit a, to La Junta, and to the entire uptown scene.

This one's for my mother,
Maricarmen Martínez,

logically.

I'm going down to Puerto Rico
I'm going down on the midnite plane
I'm going down on the Vomit Express
I'm going down with my suitcase pain.

Allen Ginsberg

Table of Contents

Nursing Home Injuries

They are breaking the dawn over faraway cities
They are babbling ecstatic trembling on rooftops
They are making faces at the cappuccino places
They are sleeping sound under cardboard stockyards
They are hurling inventory from tall tall buildings
They are counting screws on suspension bridges
They are walking hand-in-hand into the sunset crash
They are taking off their corporate underwear
They are making love to wall sockets
They are flirting with the monsters in the mirror
They are summoning the posses of thugs and priests and revelers
They are running through the traffic lights and lampposts
They are hanging from the awnings of the day that burns
They are trudging through the rivers parks and mountains
They are setting up their hammocks in dark desolate places
They are staring as the tellers lose their nametags
They are laughing on the outskirts of arrhythmia
They are washing dishes in the carjack districts
They are waiting there with bus-token-in-pocket
They are selling plantain fritters
They are wearing Urban Outfitters
They are setting fire to the skin they're in
They are spewing epithets at sexy neighbors
They are staring mirror citizens of nowhere
They are nursing home injuries
They are stockpiling pain
They are editing their telecast anxiety
They are clinging to the wreckage

They are floating somehow in a cresting sea
They are eating working growing old
They are buying groceries
They are wandering through Botox bodegas
They are floundering in homeboy boutiques
They are blending with the scenery
They are banishing the memory
They are returning home to claim the dust
They are remembering
They are vanishing breeds, touch them if you must,
They are dead starfish in a city of rust

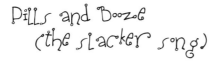

Pills and Booze
(the slacker song)

I spend my nights at home with pills and booze,
Collecting lint inside my underwear.
Occasionally I'll watch the evening news,

Unconscious in my favorite armchair.
I love those late-night ads for ab machines,
The jet stream ovens, and the spray-on hair.

I don't subscribe to glossy magazines.
I rarely bathe. They say I'm full of shit
Because I shun the literary scenes.

I'm artsy but I'm short on trust fund wit.
Each month my rent is fashionably late.
I hate a trend unless I started it.

I'm not hip to the crowds that congregate.
I do not beep or page. I screen my calls.
I like to watch the walls disintegrate.

On rainy days I wander through the malls,
In various states of sensory deprivation.
I listen to the hum of waterfalls

That emanates from distant Muzak stations.
I hang out at car washes and buffets.
I rarely read The Onion or The Nation.

I'm not a candidate for M.F.A.s.
I don't live in an ashram or a loft.
The Voice has not reviewed one of my plays.

I've never worked at Spin or Microsoft.
I own no stock and cannot ride a bike.
I like to have my nostrils Easy-Offed.

The chains, the kinky stuff—that's what I like—
The funny, random acts of violence:
The trailers overturned on the turnpike,

The kittens suffocating in the air vents,
The nursing-homers choking on a cracker.
I cultivate a solemn decadence

But in reality I'm just a slacker:
Another theorist with funky shoes,
Another hippie backpack hacky-sacker,

Another connoisseur of postpunk blues,
Another king of desktop solitaire.
I live in lonely rooms with brick wall views,

Dreaming of Oscar Wilde and Baudelaire.
I spend my nights at home with pills and booze,
Collecting lint inside my underwear.

Candy & Co.

Handing out candy
at the busy intersection
cough syrup nectar
never tasted so sweet
as when we had it
hardened
coated
wrapped
and, finally,
distributed
through the greater tri-state area
by leaking 18-wheelers

the pock-marked truckers grinned
through yellow teeth
clogging the exits
of gas stations
convenience stores
near Trenton
and snake-oil salesmen
door-to-door
pockets full of how much

     azuquita

the timelines of our private
histories
emulsified into one

glazed canvas:
the terracotta shingles on grandma's house each time we
drove there wondering what goodies would await

juicy fruit still life
of gooey fingers
groundswell of licorice
we wished would never end . . .

these days,
in keeping with market demands,
we advertise to as-of-yet
unheard-of
demographics
we cut our losses
we accept food stamps;

but those people who start food lines
in Nairobi or Bombay
will never know how far we've come
working the magic
of lollipop smiles
from the trunk of our rusty hatchback

Six Flags over Brooklyn

et de nouveau l'idylle américaine,
cataleptique
en plein soleil clair de lune

Jean Cocteau

I.   **BROOKLYN (surprise)**

red and blue flags
dancing in the distance
perhaps a used car lot
perhaps my mind busy-at-work
sliding back into its loudest gabardines;
the gutter's blackest eddies
my face refracted
to the tune of the synthesizer solos:
power ballads blasting from
the brownstone,
the sunken stone,
cans and tins clash down below

Like some sighing archeologist
I look under the lids   ("Music, maestro!")
it's all deliciously infected
infested
joyously imploding
under the heavy weight of heavy things
of heavy thighs

of prickly skin
of callous heels, toes blazin'
Baby, it is Brooklyn beckoning

II.   TIMES SQUARE (beat fantasy #1)

I wish I could reach
that fever pitch
that makes things new
and frightening
that bottles up bliss
and strategic estrangement
(the way the crooners do)
and sends it off for conspicuous
consumption
to be tagged and effectively
marketed:
"Thank God
for PowerPoint
without it we would be at sea,
our pie charts no more than
Cristoforo Colombo's
moldy withered maps.
X marks the spot.
We are the new cartographers!"
Not me,
I'm just another one of
those tired new york dolls
calling for her lover boy:
"Trash!"
rummaging thru John Ashbery's garbage
for the crust of Allen Ginsberg's sandwich throwaways,

past the big bins and heaps
behind the Times Square Sbarro
looking for my little piece of heaven
one untarnishable memento
amid the tarnished neon ladies;
they're tearing down the snuff film set
I whiff her pale marble nothingness,
looking for life,   rebirth
in the middle of the muddle

III.   **PUERTO RICO (skin effigy)**

Too long did I hang around
Puente Dos Hermanos
going bald and going native
watching the green Hyundais
heat up and wheeze
waiting for my gold-rimmed Araby
my misty Arcady
my bebop prosody
my postpunk prophecy

I watched them make their way to El Condado
tourist bars fruity drinks
nickel slot casino karaoke
and a tiny pebble
in the middle of the hazy Caribbean
goes to hell
(or better yet)
into my great-aunt Carmelita's crocodile handbag
singing salsa
will she ever be delivered from this most placid

oblivion?

Could be.

(Maybe it's not too late,
we may still be in time
to be surprised,
blindsided by the death thud of the real
like the poet counting the dead kittens,
like the prophet waiting for his beach buggy;
but there's no Puerto-Rico-of-the-mind
amid the Long—Fire—Coneys
so
it is necesario,
justo y necesario,
to invent
our own disposable
algorithms
algo ~~Something~~
lo que sea ~~Whatever~~
something similar to chance encounters
with our own breathless strokes
of fortune
so that we too may wade
(no, better yet,
be taxied off)
to shore).

IV.   SAN FRANCISCO (beat fantasy # 2)

A year farther up the road
I did wander, trampling
over the forgotten foliage
of northern California's campfire mornings,
searching for the self-made
among the ready-mades,
I got as far as nowhere
you would care to know,
lost, signaling semaphores
down the mazes of Presidio Park,
I followed that coast
by North Beach
but all I found were
the T-shirts that read
"Alcatraz Swim Team,"
danger: undertow overhead . . .

Tell me what you see:
Sunset?
Truth is
if you squint hard enough
you might just see
the last of the kids with the
gold in their hair
in their eyes:
tomorrow's brighter vistas,
quick!
before the gates drone to a close
behind them
in Atherton, California . . .

they trek across Camino
Real
with nothing but a backpack
full of trail mix
all the way to one of them
nature reserves
in the Pacific
Northwest,
where they promptly die
and here I find that words
are easily discarded
like so many of those discordant
keys
unhinged from memory's rusted xylophone
(see the repairman down below)

V.   **BROOKLYN (reprise)**

Here I am,
posing for mental Polaroids
showing the teeth of my remembrances
when I see the flags puff up once more,
smoke rises from Brooklyn's belly
above the fish markets
and kiosks full of rotten fruit.
Red and blue bellows
that point the way back
to the punchline, the refrain
goes something like this:

"then let us go tonight, my love,
to slip on banana peels

the Bards have piled up
in old wet crates,
to trip and tumble
into the bay below
and perhaps,
splashing with sea lions,
to sing again . . ."

Metal pesado 1

De pie
de moda
meciéndome en el
aluminio gastado de las
viejas capitales

te saludo del subsuelo
sin manos ni cuerpo
ni carnet—

es un amanecer turbio
para hacer turismo interior
con planchas de zinc
y pezones puncturados

te saludo al comenzar
y veamos cómo caen
las locas calcomanías
de "cómo"
y "por qué"
y "quiéreme otra vez"

Heavy Metal 1

In stride
In style
Rocking to the
Tin drums
In old capital cities

I greet you from the underground
Without hands without body
Without passport—

In this cloudy morning
We are the inner tourists
Who hide under zinc sheets
And punctured nipples,

Who meet up at the zero hour
To watch the Sun erase
The last trace of our
Comic strips cries
Without a "How"
Without a "Why"
Without a "Love me once again"

Forced Busing

"The truth is out there"
is a promise the brochures will never keep

truth is we went to Plattsburgh and it wasn't a blast
so we scurry to Albany to see the Patroons play:
during warm-up
the basketballs
thump against the rim—
and time is pressing like the
squeaking of a running shoe
on the parquet floor
so let's see something new

(the cultural logic of late capitalism
means you can't distinguish
the new from the antediluvian,
so let's camp out under the stars!
In dungarees
we'll make some s'mores
watching as the flames
consume the megastores
making the voiceless agitators and
graphic designers
blend into the stucco:
one vast expressive cultural tableau
charred beyond repair)

The truth is out there
If you can catch it:
In Mexico City it's *galgo*,
In Madrid it's *Talgo*,
In Port Authority it's *Peter Pan*,
In ghost towns of the Saratoga/Cuyahoga variety
Sites of resistance are grafts in the sand;
    . . . So we spend our Memorial Day weekends in transit
Piercing our temples imagining home
Standing in line to be born again
Under the weight of the second-hand valises
We brought with us from the long since ruined depot

LINO: Employee of the Month

The place? my favorite fast-food chain
The time? well, night, of course

(shadows and stuff)

I'm greeted by Lino,
the register rookie,
crooning "Good evening" like fresh-faced Sinatra:
"Ol' Brown Eyes plays the Burger Grill Apollo!"
yeah right.

Somewhere the black leather crowd congregates
"Line up for the line dance!
Strobe sensation! Digital drone!"

Somewhere lovers huddle crouch
cuddle
anesthetized by steady doses
of extra-strength moonshine

And I can only wonder,
could it be that sad-eyed Lino
is reading my mind as I think
"What am I doing here,
ordering onion grease and stale root beer—
expecting airy Muzak
listening instead to Bert (where's Ernie?)
do the call-and-response with the Muppet gospel choir?"

I think Lino knows better
as he slams the door behind me
mopping mayo stains
& I wish I'd hear forbidden sounds,
tap into secret signs
  tumble down trap doors
anything reminiscent of anew
in this night of watered-down rumba
with Big Bird on the bongos.

At the Palo Alto Burger King

the pretty mom asks me to proofread her paper on some Chicana feminist who was down in the dumps just like her 'til she followed that trolley to Ivy League halls . . . not a blink—is she blind?—as she goes back to force-feeding Junior mashed, oft-ketchupped fries

En los suburbios lejanos

Escucha la proclamación atroz que
Sopla en las guaridas de la nación-bosque
Vachel Lindsay

1

Mi negrita se me ha ido.
Por Dios Santo, no la encuentro—
será que se ha ido pal centro
de un downtown desconocido?
O, peor, y si es que ha sido
seducida por villanos?
o por cultos mahometanos?
Me dicen que no me ofusque,
que se perdió y que la busque
en los suburbios lejanos.

2   **Puerto Rico**

En Guaynabo y en Toa Baja
el profesor y el teórico
juegan al póker retórico
con la identidad-baraja
y se jalan otra paja
para impresionar decanos;

In the Faraway Suburbs

Listen to the creepy proclamation,
Blown through the lairs of the forest-nation

Vachel Lindsay

1

Who knows why my baby left me?
Who knows where she could have gone?
Is she hiding in the center
Of some little-known downtown?
Has she been seduced by villains?
Have they got her gagged and bound?
Vanished from the lost and found
With no trace and no reminder . . . ?
Yeah, she's lost, but I will find her
Down in the faraway suburbs.

2   **Puerto Rico**

In Guaynabo and Toa Baja
The theorists and professors
Are playing rhetorical poker
With their identity cards,
They are shooting wads of wisdom
To impress the senile deans;

y los buenos ciudadanos
trabajan para el gobierno
pegando loseta y cuerno
en los suburbios lejanos.

3   **Nueva York**

El Greyhound carga su biela
de Nueva York a Poughkeepsie
y yo voy cantando "Gypsy"
de Fleetwood Mac, a cappella,
el paisaje de acuarela
se deshace en grises planos:
los diners y los desganos
y las fábricas desiertas
y el rechinar de las puertas
en los suburbios lejanos.

4

Hay esqueletos prehistóricos
en la playa en Staten Island
y las aguavivas bailan
lentos valses hidroclóricos,
chalets con detalles dóricos
y sirvientes bolivianos
donde juegan los hermanos
a oler sobaco y solventes,
y el perro muestra sus dientes
en los suburbios lejanos.

Meanwhile, the good citizens
Are all working for the government,
Cheating on taxes and spouses
Down in the faraway suburbs.

3   **New York**

The Greyhound wheezes its way
From New York up to Poughkeepsie;
I pass the time singing "Gypsy"
By Fleetwood Mac, a cappella;
And the watercolor landscape
Falls apart on the gray planes;
The diners and the dead-ends,
The deserted factories,
And the doors creak noisily
Down in the faraway suburbs.

4

There are prehistoric skeletons
At the beach on Staten Island
And the jellyfish are dancing
Slow, hydrochloric waltzes;
There are Doric-style chalets
With South American servants
Where the little brothers play;
Sniffing underarms and solvents
While the dog shows off its teeth
Down in the faraway suburbs.

5

Al final de la autopista
se abren bosques medievales
hay centros correccionales
y un McDonald's sin turistas—
me sobrecoge la vista:
las mansiones en los llanos,
los projects y los gusanos
del enorme vertedero
en fuego una noche de enero
en los suburbios lejanos.

6   **California**

En los vecindarios regios,
Atherton, West Palo Alto,
pavimentan el asfalto
con brea de privilegios—
suenan sólo los arpegios
de los pregrabados pianos
y ese temblar de las manos
que se sirven su ginebra
hasta que el vaso se quiebra
en los suburbios lejanos.

5

Here the end of the expressway
Gives way to medieval forests
And correctional facilities
And McDonald's without tourists;
I'm overwhelmed by the view
Of the mansions on the plains,
The housing projects, the flames
Creeping through the dead of winter
As the landfill burns tonight
Down in the faraway suburbs.

6   **California**

In the righteous neighborhoods,
Atherton, West Palo Alto,
They're paving over the asphalt
With the gravel of privilege—
All one hears are the arpeggios
Of the pre-recorded pianos,
And the trembling of the hands
That are serving themselves gin
And the shot glass shattering
Down in the faraway suburbs.

7

Lejos de los arrabales,
en Millbrae y en Redwood City,
otro neighborhood committee
crea centros comunales
y moles monumentales
para los placeres sanos:
softbol peewee los veranos,
window-shopping, Cineplex,
batidas de fruta Tex-Mex
en los suburbios lejanos.

8

Un Sol distante y magnífico
lame los acantilados,
busco tu ojo engominado
en la costa del Pacífico.
Marin County en específico
tiene fantasmas urbanos,
saxofonistas enanos
que añoran días de gloria
y ahora cuentan su historia
en los suburbios lejanos.

7

Far from all the shantytowns,
In Millbrae and Redwood City,
One more neighborhood committee
Is creating civic centers
And more monumental malls
Catering to healthy pleasures:
Peewee softball in the summers,
Window-shopping, Cineplex,
And those fruity Tex-Mex shakes
Down in the faraway suburbs.

8

A distant, majestic Sun
Licks the cliffs and the embankments,
I search for your embalmed eye
On the coast of the Pacific.
Marin County in particular
Has its share of urban ghosts,
Like those midget saxophonists
Who long for their days of glory
And are now telling their story
Down in the faraway suburbs.

9

Te he buscado en cada esquina
del inocuo continente
será que te tengo de frente?
que te tengo de vecina?
que el downtown y la gomina
y la mugre de tus manos
son hologramas arcanos?
que tu promesa epiléptica
murió esa noche antiséptica
en los suburbios lejanos.

9

I've searched for you in each corner of
This innocuous continent—
Could it be you're facing me?
Could it be that you're my neighbor?
That the downtown and the eye balm
And the grime that coats your hands
Are all arcane holograms?
That your epileptic smile
Died that antiseptic night
Down in the faraway suburbs.

Dreaming,

the pretty boy fumbles in the dark
for my change purse.
I can see the Super 8
it all looks sepia
I chase him down Madrid
past punks in Malasaña
down calle Luis de Góngora,
my high heels clunking in the
cobblestones
and then he fades to black.

Here the phone wakes me up:
it's mom. She says she loves me barrelfuls.
I wonder what she meant.
Now I hang up. My turn to fade.

Sour Grapes

Aloof,
deprogrammed,
the irony is that we are human.

In the unity of a group
or divided into subgroups
they will engage
when they accept—
happy for
those for whom the fold
of reasoning
parallels the reply
of mathematicians
who, when asked
what they believe,
 say,
"Tell me who you've seen,
tell me about the dance."

The strobe lights with a small charge,
it frequently happens that the same house
which one person built, at a vast expense,
is neglected by another—
or so the story goes . . .

The dance
was at the farm house
where the war veterans met.

"Grapes are lucrative
and regulations are well established,"
mumbled the blind admiral,
to no one in particular.

"Check out the vines,
twisted early in the morning,
stretching far and wide—
soon I'll own the interstate!"

He twirled his plastic machete.
He wanted to get back—fast!—
and set the idle girls to some work
that would fill their wandering heads.

Until he heard the crash.

"It sure sounds like thunder,
though I don't know what it means . . .
maybe it's a truck . . . ,"
he pondered,
unaware that it was already night.

The moon dripped pale contempt—
so that the blind admiral,
preso da ardore guerrero,
misi il lume in mano
au moment où montaient les ombres . . .

The last of the tambourines played out.

Bientôt il faudra partir:

un petit peu de frivolités,
l'horrible soif
e todos com muito medo
foram correndo pra fora,   (there they was)
stumbling toward the main road,
timeless getaway!

The young newlyweds snapped pictures from afar,
hooting,
acting like the press,
waving from the overpass,
blinking, honking the rental car.

He cleared a patch of crabgrass . . .
where was that place,   he wondered,
where angels break off
from the living metal,
far from the wear & tear
of improperly adjusted
or maintained drives?

It is bad enough to feel
the dream-like force,
a Machiavellian impulse,
a churning,
same time, same place, next year.

For now there's enough
droplets on the pane,
a gray parade
of anemones
plucked intact from memory,
awash on the faraway shore

Lost and Found in Taksim Square

To my good friends at the Madrid Bar, Istanbul

I'm turning off my TV set
I'm tired of spectating [No. I'm tired of participating...]
Are you tired too?

[are these things so different?]

Then come chase me through the minarets
Down to the reddish shore

I'll take you up the hill
To a place that knows no borders,
A place that's free from the dogma of fun,
A place to be sharp and dense and formless
Like the smoke that rises
From the Bosphorus this morning

If you miss me,
I'll be sitting at the far end of the bar,
Hearing sound spin,
Filling my head full of soccer statistics and
Beer-soaked politics,
Misquoting Byzantine mystics
While rain falls and the world outside
Gets peeled of its ugly death gauze.
So let us pause here, you and I,
Far from the duty-free laissez-faire crowd,
For we've reached someplace important,
Imposing as the city walls that flank us.

[away from the spaces of the market and into alcoholic stupor]

The men line up at the market
This morning, ready to sell us
More useless souvenirs:
Mosque magnets,
Maps of Istanbul in Braille *exploitation of*
And a small, metallic garbage pail *a real need*
Used by Mohammed himself.

But if you drop your suitcase
And come away with me
We'll leave behind the tourist traps,
The fuzzed-out fascism of today's
Romantic comedy of choice.

The future looks sad but true. And therefore funny.
And therefore full of hope.
So drop your misgivings like more lost luggage.
For I have seen the sunrise.
Over the empty square:
Commodity culture with its
Tacky makeup and its heels
Offers me a quick thrill
And slithers back into the alley
But I am not impressed—
I have seen a better place:
Our friends are waiting there with open arms
In that railway
Into the heart of the real.

Magnets

Despair
smashed.
Tasted.

Can stars decay?

Us,
Unhooked, travel?

And I,
fruit of blue
years past,

time gated and
despair unlocked,

trip over you and smile?

The Pragmatist

Day after day
norm 9 to 5 (or 6 or midnight), *reality*
a cartoon hunchback
in a cut-out cubicle
humming mindless Muzak,
typing mindless memos
to remind his mindless boss
of his mindless meetings
in mindless bistros
full of mindless waiters
and the mindlessness of
so much minestrone
slurped alone or in
the company of corporate drones
who throw him a bone
and make him work overtime for free
'cause he's temp-to-perm
but I hear the firm has
its eye on him.

He puts on his fake moustache
and goes to work.
He won't get promoted
He won't leave this cubicle
He'll never slide into the comfortable tedium of success
He'll never buy his mom that house
He'll never vacation in the placid reflux of the Hamptons,
or get lost in the mindrot Rivieras
with a bunch of executive asshole buddies

in a state of joyous, drugged-out mindlessness
scoring with the babe of his dreams.

He will, however, get full benefits. Including top-notch health
coverage from a leading HMO. It even includes dental!

Herald square, 6 PM

Loose shoelaces plucked
in unison, form new fugues
for a fading day

Grand Mal

He is trying to keep it together—He walks up to the drugstore window and pleads his case—They will have none of it: ". . . not without a prescription; it's store policy"—By the time he plops back down on the park bench he is going in and out of consciousness: first an aura, a foreboding, a strange smell, a series of flashing lights, shifting geometric patterns, then a jolt to the back of the head, a lightning bolt—

The passersby [try not to stare] just grab their coiffured dogs, pick [at the] falafel sandwiches, make sure their designer watches are still there, [wound], and walk away—

Soon the tingling will subside and all he'll hear is these piped-in E-Z listening drones: the cell phones generating static? the sounds of turbines? cycles of birth and death? seasons collapsing? . . . or just another mindless afternoon in the industrial park?

Word Is Saving Agneta

Why do I treasure stasis?
why are the sound systems haywire
where you are, Agneta,
that you don't see the four-way stop?
the choice is yours, babe
be mine
be pummeled by the apes in charge
another tutu squad
another cutesy masquerade
where are you going gun-in-hand?
hey, Joe shot his lady and you shot your mouth
down south
down Mexicali way

Agneta I gave you the gun
because your residue in me
is long-lasting cornpone,
stubborn like turpentine
but there are bridges uncrossable
and perhaps it's those, babe,
where it's best to push the next guy
aside
to fold him up   square
knot   send offffff
way down south
where all be free;
ee!   celebr
888888888888888

asking me for it
but I have not seen it,
last I heard it busy-bodied its way
up some bucolic nook
in the Great
Alp-like
Smoky
Sierras
where we rocked—
that piece of ass
where are it?   where, Ag, did you take it?
the one
1111111111111111
my toothless   my
titless   my
glandular Agneta,
heaven is too much for   you
perhaps
but then again you're just too much
a starry climb to moon
axing one's way to the torrid climes
in stinky marmot fur
in plain view of the truth
living off no faith
we may speak of
whale oil!

Open to be forked
rimmed hand-
jobbed by
the first curious
passerby

to clamp his yellow
arthritic
paw

in elegy:
the Negro blowtorch
played the blue guitar acid
sparks and you
unwinding
into sin—
lechery
leprosy
whatever—
sin
mere synecdoche
for glass tidings past and yet to arrive

                    (   )

there are mansions in colonial Williamsborough
where the doctors can't get to
because it's too wild
shrubbery   jungle   vine
transit   bamboo   bramble
can't stand next to the mountain
burning;
memorial estate cystitis
is a-flare
where they mourn your parting
their cankers, yep,
the consequence
of your having not
as of yet arrived . . .

because
you bring glad tidings
and then I tidy up
Glad bag disarray
goodbye,
let it go over the rapids
in plain view of men
in mass transit stations
desolate
chap stick
underarm
repellent
tampons
trampled by the tracks
of our love

Quicksand

I once knew a fellow from Spicland
Who fell from America's kickstand:
He'd crawled past the border
With dreams made to order
The beautiful color of quicksand.

tantilizing trap

Liquidación

por la avenida de los
almendros muertos
todo está calmado
y si el cielo está abollado
es porque me comí la luna anoche

ahora queda el agujero
donde vacío la tómbola
o mente, que es lo mismo—
oigan,

sólo suenan los panderos
que llevo amarrados al lomo,

felizmente mi palabra hierve
y se pierde en la noche—
total, da igual,
pues el tronco del árbol que cayó
ya más nunca nos servirá de puente

es que ya no hay nada de qué hablar

salir de nuevo
del trabajo a la casa,
solo y sonriente,

de vuelta a mis panderos,
ciudadano apenas

Clearance

All is calm today
Along the avenue
Where the dead almond trees lie
And if the sky is dented,
Hey, it's because I ate the moon last night

All that's left is the hole
Where I empty the tumbler
Of my mind,
Listen,

You can hear the tambourines
That dangle from my back,

Happily my words boil over
And blend into the night—
Anyhow, it makes no difference,
Since the trunk of the tree that fell
Can no longer be our bridge

Because there's nothing left to talk about

To go again
From job to house,
Alone and smiling,

Back to my tambourines
Barely a citizen

de una música interna.
he borrado las caras de las fotos,
ya más nunca nos veremos de frente

Of an inner music.
I have erased the faces of the photos,
Never again will we see eye to eye

A Fence

The blind tides are here
and who is keeping track of the weather?

The days are flooded
awash in ash
a template for suspicion

The tablet is afloat.
Among the dead we sit
decoding a forgotten alphabet,
a stare

The eyes of the child
lie,
because he has been
fed his lines like milk
with chocolate

There is a fence
here. It is made of hair
and star
and voices hushed
then hurried into
love

Kool Logic

The Cultural Logic of Late Capitalism

Fredric Jameson

1

same

I hope this finds you in good health
(Or at least gainfully employed).
We're here to discuss the hologram-self   *imagined self / commodity*
In the era of the void.

Some say modern man is hollow,
Others say it's a condition
Called "postmodern." Do you follow?
Could this use some exposition?   *Quatrains*

2

O.K. See the common graves
Rotting in the ancient cities?
The fast food? The porous borders?   *stanza*
The ambiguous sexualities?   *separation*
is openness a quagmire?
is there still hierarchy & sexism
The debt-bludgeoned ethnicities?
The wars of chemical roses?
Cash flows from Utopian rivers
And the market never closes!
   This is the kool logic
   Of late capitalism.

52

La Lógica kool

The Cultural Logic of Late Capitalism

Fredric Jameson

1

Cantémosle al día mítico
de identidad-holograma,
quince minutos de fama
(veinte si eres político);
ya salió el sol sifilítico
en el pabellón sombrío
de la era del vacío,
lanza su luz desigual:
    la lógica cultural
    del capitalismo tardío.

2

Filas de comunes fosas
en las ciudades antiguas,
sexualidades ambiguas,
fast food, fronteras porosas,
guerras de químicas rosas,
etnias que escurren rocío
y la utopía es un río
que vomita capital:
    la lógica cultural
    del capitalismo tardío.

3

[handwritten: mental health market]

In the Prozac marketplaces
People hoard new modes of leisure;
Love has been deregulated:
Plastic breasts! Prosthetics! Seizures!

In the suburbs neighbors mourn
The death drive of their libidos,
Late summers full of soft porn,
Stolen Wonderbras, torn Speedos.
    This is the kool logic
    Of late capitalism.

4

You can consume what you please:
From world music to new age;
Ricky Martin and John Cage
Are touring the Basque Pyrenees;

You can sing your songs of peace   *[handwritten: music is comodified]*
(Pop! Punk! Folk! Tribal! Assorted!)
But the violence will not cease,
Hate's fetus can't be aborted!
    This is the kool logic
    Of late capitalism.

3

El amor desregulado
por nuevos medios de ocio,
senos plásticos, negocio
de prótesis, Prozac, mercado,
eros suburbanizado,
pornografías de estío
como geishas de Darío
en flujo libidinal:
    la lógica cultural
    del capitalismo tardío.

4

Cada cual lo que le plazca,
música-mundo, new age,
Ricky Martin y John Cage
de gira por Tierra Vasca—
que el feto del odio nazca
de la hojarasca de hastío,
nueva trova, power trío,
queer punk, flamenco tribal:
    la lógica cultural
    del capitalismo tardío.

5

Macrobiotic-cybernetic-
Fiber-optic folderol!
Neo-gothic supermodels!
Satellites and virtual malls!
Vegan power lunch grand slams!
Word Elites! Money-go-rounds!
Free will or free (pillow?) shams
In the global shantytown?
    This is the kool logic
    Of late capitalism.

6

NAFTA, Mercosur, Hamas!
DVDs and open mikes!
Watercress and motocross!
SUVs and mountain bikes!

Trailer parks! Gated communities!
Highrise ghettoes and favelas!
Acquired diplomatic immunities!
Self-help prophets! Braille novellas!

Mexico, Miami, Río!
Euro-Disney, Bollywood!
Dell, Intel, Taco Bell, Geo!
Stanford post-docs in da hood!

5

Cibernéticoestrambótico,
macrobióticoinformáticas,
supermodelos hieráticas,
geografías de lo erótico,
lo ecológico y lo gótico,
satélite, elite, mall frío,
simulacro o albedrío
en el chinchorro global:
   la lógica cultural
   del capitalismo tardío.

6

NAFTA, Mercosur, o sea
Baudrillard y Lipovetsky,
el sports utility, el jet ski,
comunidad europea,
Hollywood Hills y La Brea,
D.F., Miami Beach, Río,
la favela, el caserío
y esta fiebre sin final:
   la lógica cultural
   del capitalismo tardío.

I'll stop fronting pedagogical . . .
One last question (extra credit):
This kool logic ain't too logical
But it's still "kool." Do you get it?!

> This is the kool logic
> Of late capitalism.

Still Life

under the burnt car moon
fast down Bushwick Avenue;
we're yesterday's cartoons
over tall tall grass—like vacant
mindscapes, skipping the
discordant note
of muted cities until
color and sound merge
until color and merge
until merge
m
e   r
     g
      e

Doble tanda

Y después de todo
te atreves llamarle ciudad
a este cubo compacto de desilusiones

la llave de paso que te abrió la mente
te llena el cráneo de arena
y mares de miradas desviadas

lo cierto es que despiertas
en parques
y plazas
indagando, tembloroso, el porqué de las cosas

todavía sueñas, con babas en la boca,
con salir de madrugada al rompeolas,
ser tonto y libre y flotar hacia las boyas;

pero queda claro
que has visto demasiado,
sabes lo que te espera.   tarde.
un primer acto fingido,
sólo el diálogo   ha sido improvisado

así como la parte en que oyes venir el tren
y duermes bajo el sol,
amarrado a los rieles,
y nadie aplaude cuando
se te derriten las sienes

Double Feature

And after all
You look at this compact crate
Of disappointments and
Dare call it a city

The passkey that opened your mind
Fills your cranium with sand
And a sea of swerving glances

The fact is that you wake up
In parks
And squares
Trembling, searching for the meaning of things

You still dream, as drool drips from your mouth,
Of heading out to the breakwater at dawn,
Of being dumb and free and floating toward the buoys;

But it is clear
That you have seen too much,
You know what awaits you.   late.
A faked first act,
Only the dialogue   has been improvised

As well as the part where you hear the train coming
And you sleep under the sun,
Tied to the rails,
And nobody applauds
When your temples start to melt

Barrio Speedwagon Blues

I.

There's melting pots sofriendo
Masitas de muchedumbre
Y tengo la mala costumbre
Del que sonríe sufriendo;
So I stare outside my window
At the rats who pay their dues
Down abandoned avenues;
Varios diarios relicarios
De vecindarios precarios . . .
Barrio Speedwagon Blues!

II.

I don't mind the daily walk,
De nuevo nursing the nightmare,
I'm happy just going nowhere,
Fast-track dreams in laughtrack shock,
I wear the street's scar, just like Prufrock,
In the crater of my shoes,
In the sunset's purple bruise,
Under street lamps sin que alumbre
Mi cómica pesadumbre . . .
Barrio Speedwagon Blues!

III.

I've learned all my civics lessons
In this republic of deadpan,
Emptied out my mental bedpan
With Zen and antidepressants;
Now I'm stuck-in-convalescence
Y se me quiebra la cruz,
Y me acuerdo when we'd cruise
Down the coast, nursing home injuries,
Singing our song of lost centuries:
Barrio Speedwagon Blues!

IV.

I'm too old to take a ride
In a rented chrome machine
Down the freeways and ravines
Hurling my pain to the tides;
Now my autism collides
With the headlines on the news
And my lovers say I snooze
En depresión atmosférica,
But I still dream of America . . .
Barrio Speedwagon Blues!

V.

Esta ciudad es un empate
Entre alcaldes billonarios
Y activistas solidarios
Atop a corporate mattress;
But I'd never knock the Rat Race
'Cause my blood cannot refuse
Its internal revenues
De burgués y de atorrante
Y el que la sepa que cante:
Barrio Speedwagon Blues!

VI.

Esta canción no se acaba;
Gimme a sec and I'll finish it,
I'll spew out some funny shit,
Metaliterary baba;
So drop your joint and your java,
Stop scribbling those curlicues
Parce que maintenant j'accuse . . . !
Slumming days away like Dreyfus:
Why does all this feel so lifeless?
Barrio Speedwagon Blues!

Next Exit

To live now is to break the glass
in blood and
give it back as love

To stand courageously
in a one-inch shaft of light
mostly letting off emotional overflows

To claim as yours
the power to disappear

To push the wheelbarrow
across the empty field and hum
as the birds melt into the night.

To see the last of you
latching onto a handful of dust,
colliding with hope
as death loops its own laughtrack

To live now is to face that road
where music turns to static
and wind slices skin,
trying to forget,
trying to begin

Vacant Blues

I swallow a pill but there is no cure
A city map won't get me where I want to go

Scaling the scaffold,
mindless of the mall,
unaware of driveways
where housewives dodge the wrecking ball,
I crawl outside these vacant blues

and into the contours of your eyes

Greetings From the Upper West Side of My Burning Brain

In this new place nobody knows me
The neighbors harbor suspicions
That I splash the dirty toilet water
Until it overflows into the streets,
Which would account for the black puddles
Down the grease-stained avenue

Like a paranoid porter
I wear a hat over my face
To shield me from the footsteps
Of unwanted guests, but I'm still one of
These people walking every day
To and from the store
To and from the job
To and from the matinee
That kills them with a laugh.
I laugh too, in the last row,
But only because I have memorized the lines
Of that silly script. The last scene is the best,
Where the girl with the "great ass"
Says "This is my country" and proceeds
To dynamite the federal building.

Soon the people will walk out, remembering
Embers, squinting under the late summer sun
And they will not see me as I pass,
I'm mumbling about "community"
But I'm not sure I'm a part of the same movie.

Truth is
This new place is an odd place
To live out my urban coolcat fantasies.
The upper west side, the real one,
Has no mascara-seeping Palm Pilot Senior Citizens,
No sexy theorists walking their designer dogs,
Just a parade of brothers in wifebeaters
Huddled by the parking meters
And lovely wilted waitresses
Filling out time cards

And yet we're all a part of the parade (maybe enough)
With our check in the mail and
Our highrise ideals,
Running from the guard dogs' political paws
Heading home to the sofa/fridge no-brain-zone
to shut the door and sleep and then begin again.

El hombre lobo

Doy vueltas al parque abandonado,
El zafacón está lleno de moscas,
No hay luz—puede que no me reconozcas—
Las babas se me salen por el lado
De la boca. Yo no soy de su agrado,
Más bien insisto, como bestias toscas
Al arado. Y colecciono roscas
De ésas que se salen del alumbrado,
De aquéllas que caen de los rascacielos
Y espío amores tras de las cortinas
Y algunos cuerpos me sirven de velos—
Es más simple de lo que te imaginas:
Te maldigo! Mis ojos son anzuelos
Para exhumar tu corazón en ruinas.

Death and Taxes

The housewives laugh at what they can't avoid:
In single file, buckling one by one
Under the weight of the late summer sun,
They drop their bags, they twitch, and are destroyed.
He hears a voice (there is a bust of Freud
Carved on the mountainside). He tucks the gun
Under his rented beard and starts to run.
("The housewives laugh at what they can't avoid.")
Like She-bears fettered to a rusted moon
They crawl across the parking lot and shed
Tearblood. The office park is closing soon.
Night falls. The neighborhood buries its dead
And changes channels—Zap! Ah, the purity
Of death and taxes and Social Security.

Spic Tracts

I'm the Puerto Rican
Whose dad is a gringo
Whose mom is a Platonist
Whose pain won't buy plátanos
Who drinks toasted almond
Who can't speak the lingo
Who made it to Stanford
Without knowing Windows
except for the ones on this
car service soapbox
that takes me uptown
thru the storefronts of a foreign land
houses of ancestors I don't recognize.

I've got no friends named Papo
who hang around street corners
"Vaya, mami" and *"Boricua one hundred*
                              per-
cent,
represent!"

> Don't even have a car
> to wash on Sunday afternoons
> away those NY/PR blues
> no homeboy convoy to loot Loisaida
> listening to la Fania
> salsa vieja por mi madre por la radio

Without no toothless grandma
in El barrio
choking on those mounds
of freeze-dried mofongo
the way it never was
because my real grandma
pops Xanax in the suburbs
and dreams of final hours
a whitewash apocalypse to do
away with viral strip mall cosmos.

I spend the summers at my aunt's
in Hialeah,
I'm not down with the program
and I never met Mumia
still,
I have a past

It just doesn't have me—
I have an ethnicity
          in halves
Yeah, the big city
curiosity
ani-
     fuckin'-
mosity . . .

And now a jazz interlude . . .
I've got me a bebop prosody
A jazzbo poesy
A free form soapbox sound off,
But only 'cause I can't sing
"Paranoid" and blow your slacker brains out

be patient, I'm turning the corner

Don Quijote,
when backed into a corner,
told the fuzz
"Yo sé quién soy":
I know who I am.

   Truth was he didn't
   as he charged,
   spear-in-hand,
   to get the bad guys boned and gutted—
   and neither do I
   with my hand down my pants
   and neither do you,
   papi paid for you to live under the bridge,
   mother nature for a fridge,
   you tell me how *proud* you are
   your *heritage*
      ("ven Mamá, ven Tití:
      look at the scars of my victim identity!")

   I knew you were reekin'
   In your poets café
   So I covered my nose
   And left you with the hobos.

   If it's true that the masses are asses
   then the poet is their wipe

the best pages are always dirty from life
make ya dizzy from the vapors,
(think of Mayakovsky mooning at the bay,

Pablo de Rokha injecting his telegraphy of hope)
they knew there never was no garden
In the beginning we were all full of it
When we ate the apple it was candy-coated crap,

So whoever amongst you is pure
may he cast the first stone
or get stoned
and go home
'cause I know where you live,
but I'm not selling this sermon door-to-door.

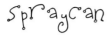

Spraycan

I wrote my name against the wall
the spray can let out a long and shapeless hiss
that was the sound of my collision
with the anonymous metropolis

The Wayside Story

And after that a darkness
Heavier than lead,
All full of writing things
And ineffectual vomitings
And voices wailing, wailing,
We are damned and dead!

Salomón de la Selva

1

Once upon a time I dreamed
Of a heroic exile,
So I fled my native isle—
Million miles (or so it seemed)—
In my eyes the moonlight gleamed
Like some brine-tinged astrolabe
'Til a huge white-crested wave
Toppled me into the sea . . .
Hip-hip: the land of the free!
Hooray: the home of the brave!

2

In despair I praised the Lord,
Jesus, Dalai Lama, Mommy!
See me through this stark tsunami!
But my pleas went on ignored;
So I latched onto a board

(Driftwood? Well, sure beats the grave!),
Could some buried currents save
A soul afloat, aloof, at sea? . . .
Hip-hip: the land of the free!
Hooray: the home of the brave!

3

Didn't need no gear for scuba,
I just swam like an amphibian
All the way through the Caribbean
From Port-au-Prince to Aruba.
Gloria Estefan croons "Skip Cuba!"
(Her chords crack at every octave),
Yo, fish, watch me move groove rave,
I reach shores lined with debris . . .
Hip-hip: the land of the free!
Hooray: the home of the brave!

4

A one-man intrepid commando,
My hands all trembling and clammy,
I crawl to some beach called Miami
(On the waterfront, like Brando!)
Pluto guides me to Orlando,
Epcot, if I scrounge and save
I can see the world's a cave
Lit by gringo shopping spree . . .
Hip-hip: the land of the free!
Hooray: the home of the brave!

5

I dream of nights in white satin
(Fashion fabric boxer itch),
Hurry up this Greyhound bitch
And drop me off in Manhattan;
Call me hippie, queer, and Latin,
But keep me rent stabilized, babe;
'Cause a ritzy yuppie enclave
Has no room for bums like me . . .
Hip-hip: the land of the free!
Hooray: the home of the brave!

6

It's not hard to sell your heart
For a penny sale at J.C.'s
I'm crazy with dreams of Macy's
But I can make do with Wal-Mart
Bloated brimful shopping cart
Mom and Pop's store kissed the grave
Heartland hopes too late to stave (off)
This big business jamboree . . .
Hip-hip: the land of the free!
Hooray: the home of the brave!

7

Army won't mind, they'll enlist me
Though I'm ethnically ambiguous,
N.R.A. just call me big wuss
Then they shoot (just barely missed me!);

Preacher says Christ would've kissed me
Except I'm a bum: "He gave
His soul for *ours* to save—
Not *yours*! Scram, smelly hillbilly!" . . .
Hip-hip: the land of the free!
Hooray: the home of the brave!

8

Puerto Rico, China, Chile,
Santo Domingo, El Salvador,
Pakistan, Mexico, Ecuador
Each exports its own hillbilly
Just like me, so quaint, so silly,
In dire need of a fix (a shave?)—
"Leave your pigsties! Smile! Behave!"
Thunders Lady Liberty . . .
Hip-hip: the land of the free!
Hooray: the home of the brave!

9

Each hillbilly to his ghetto
Where he takes all fate can dish up,
Back to the wall, like a bishop,
Cornered, skewered, can't fianchetto.
Yep, thus reads this tramp's libretto:
Looks depraved, then starts to rave,
Leaves New York for L.A. shockwave.
Drug thug death bug? No siree! . . .
Hip-hip: the land of the free!
Hooray: the home of the brave!

10

Tinseltown buzz kept me manic
On my toes, alive and hyper
But fate fired a dead-on sniper,
Luck broke down (I'm no mechanic!):
They re-christened me "Hispanic,"
Latin Tex-Mex Carib babe,
Illegal immigrant slave?
Migrant working slob? Not me! . . .
Hip-hip: the land of the free!
Hooray: the home of the brave!

11

All it took? One rubberstamping!
"Fill that oval, check that box,
Here's to you, Señor Hard Knocks
And your tribe's racial revamping!
Adiós, good ol' days of tramping
Nameless rootless tumbling knave,
Now it's spic time: dance! behave!
Clean them toilets span and spic, Sí? . . .
Hip-hip: the land of the free!
Hooray: the home of the brave!

12

Mine's no privileged bel canto,
Me be hooked on cacophonics
Caught between imposed Ebonics
And insipid Esperanto,

Oh Lord, cuánto cuánto cuánto?
How long must I feel a slave
To coos and croons? . . . it's as if they've
Written out my lines for me:
"Say, 'Hip-hip: land of the free!'—
Sing, 'Hooray: home of the brave!' "

13

Sick of tight-assed culture quotas
In a white-washed PC planet,
I traverse the globe, I span it
From Dakar to the Dakotas:
Igloos, mud huts, slums, pagodas,
"Enjoy Coke" signs, streamlined enclaves,
Golden Arches, quick bar car craves—
Sing in global irony:
Hip-hip: the land of the free!
Hooray: the land of the brave!

14

Those who know claim God is dead
But I'm not much into deicide,
I'll just lay down by the wayside
With a dung heap for a bed
And I'll break the moldy bread
And I'll face the final wave
And now, fixing for a crave,
A whim a way a why a we . . .
Hip-hip: the land of the free!
Hooray: the home of the brave!